INTRODUCTION TO
SYRIAN PERSONAL STATUS AND FAMILY LAW

INTRODUCTION TO
SYRIAN PERSONAL STATUS AND FAMILY LAW

Syrian Legislation and Jurisprudence on Marriage, Divorce, Custody, Guardianship and Adoption for the Purpose of Immigration to the United States

Ibrahim Ghabour, Esq.

JuraLaw

Introduction to Syrian Personal Status and Family Law: Syrian Legislation and Jurisprudence on Marriage, Divorce, Custody, Guardianship and Adoption for the Purpose of Immigration to the United States

Ibrahim Ghabour, Esq.

2017 Edition

ISBN (13) (paperback): 978-1-68109-082-5
ISBN (10) (paperback): 1-68109-082-1
ISBN (13) (ePub): 978-1-68109-083-2
ISBN (10) (ePub): 1-68109-083-X

JuraLaw

an imprint of TellerBooks™

t TellerBooks

www.TellerBooks.com/JuraLaw

Self-Help Guides to the Law™

Self-Help Guides to the Law™ explain the law in clear, concise terms to a popular audience of non-lawyers. Summarizing the key areas of the law with which readers are most likely to come into contact, the *Guides* broadly outline the statutes and cases that govern immigration law, landlord-tenant relations, personal injury, contracts, family law, criminal law and constitutional law and procedure.

With detailed references to sources for readers wishing to delve deeper, the *Guides* are ideal for readers wishing to better understand their legal rights and responsibilities, regardless of whether they ultimately opt to hire a lawyer.

About the Imprint

With a focus on international and comparative law, the JuraLaw™ imprint publishes monographs exploring public and private international law and overviews of the laws of various nations.

JuraLaw

SUMMARY CONTENTS

DETAILED CONTENTS

DETAILED CONTENTS

CHAPTER I. INTRODUCTION TO THE SYRIAN LEGAL SYSTEM

A. HISTORY OF SYRIAN LAW

The legal system of Syria has experienced vast changes in its composition and construct over the course of a history dating back millenniums. As Syria has been occupied by peoples as ancient as the Canaanites and Phoenicians, to, in more modern times, the Ottoman Turks and the French,[1] both the form of government over Syria, as well as Syria's laws, have experienced dramatic changes.

At present, Syria's legal system is based on an amalgam of Islamic law and French and Ottoman civil law.[2] These legal systems are the vestiges of the Syrian occupation by various groups, first the Arab Muslims, who occupied Syria in 636 AD, then the Ottoman Turks, who conquered Syria in 1517, and then finally the French, who held Syria as a French mandate by a decree of the League of Nations in 1922.

---

[1] Bureau of Near Eastern Affairs, U.S. Department of State, "Background Note: Syria," available at http://www.state.gov/r/pa/ei/bgn/3580.htm.

[2] Central Intelligence Agency, "Syria," *The World Factbook*, available at https://www.cia.gov/library/publications/the-world-factbook/geos/sy.html.

During the French occupation of Syria, pressures exerted by Syrian nationalist groups for a period of over twenty years were at times met by a heavy pushback by the French. These pressures came to a head in the mid-1940s, and the French were forced to evacuate their troops in 1946. On April 17, 1946, Syria declared its independence and was left to rule itself under a republican government formed during the French mandate.

Upon receiving independence, Syria experienced a series of upheavals and military coups. On March 8, 1963, the Arab Socialist Resurrection Party (Ba'ath Party) took over and installed leftist Syrian Army officers over the nation's executive and legislative powers. On November 13, 1970, Defense Minister Hafez al-Assad succeeded in a bloodless military coup in what was known as the Correction Movement and assumed the role of prime minister.

In March 1973, parliamentary elections for the People's Council were held and the current Syrian Constitution went into effect. According to the Constitution of 1973, which continues to apply until this day, the Syrian Arab Republic is a democratic, popular, socialist and sovereign state with a republican system of government. The Constitution establishes Islamic jurisprudence (فقه) as a main source of legislation. Specifically, it is the *hanafi* school (مذهب الحنفي) of Sunni Islamic jurisprudence that is applied in Syria. If ever the case arises where a judge must make a decision where there is no legislation on point, he may apply the relevant Islamic jurisprudence.[3]

B. JUDICIAL SYSTEM IN SYRIA

Two separate judicial systems operate in Syria: (i) a system of secular courts for matters of civil and criminal law; and (ii) a system of religious courts for matters of personal status. There are three levels of courts: Courts of First Instance (trial courts), Courts of Appeals, and the Court of Cassation, which is the highest authority on the judicial pyramid.[4] Furthermore, the Syrian Constitution provides for a Constitutional Court, which handles mostly constitutional law matters, but may handle other matters, such as issues relating to electoral law.[5]

1. Secular Courts

The secular courts in Syria are divided into the Courts of General Jurisdiction and the Administrative Courts. The Courts of General Jurisdiction are separated into six branches, all of which are further categorized by Civil and

---

[3] Interview with Yamman Samman, attorney in private practice in Damascus, Syria. 10 November 2010.

[4] Unclassified Damascus Briefing 00000657, VZCZCXYZ0000, RR RUEHWEB. FM American Embassy Damascus. E.O. 13526.

[5] *Id.*

Penal Chambers (with the exception of the Personal Status Courts). These branches are: (i) The Court of Cassation; (ii) Courts of Appeal; (iii) Tribunals of First Instance; (iv) Tribunals of Peace; (v) Personal Status Courts; and (vi) Courts for Minor Offendors.[6]

The Court of Cassation is the highest court of General Jurisdiction and hears appeals from the lower courts and can overturn judgments rendered by Courts of Appeal in criminal and civil cases. The Courts of Appeal each preside over a separate governorate (محافظات) and are divided into Civil and Penal Chambers. Each Court of Appeal hears appeals of decisions in cases previously tried before the Tribunals of First Instance and the Tribunals of Peace.

There are several Tribunals of First Instance located in each governorate. Each Tribunal is divided into several divisions according to nature of the cases presented:

- The Tribunals of Peace preside over minor civil and criminal matters and are abundant in each governorate.
- The Personal Status Courts deal mostly in personal status and family matters and vary according to the religion and ethnic origin of the litigants.

---

[6] Info-Prod Research (Middle East) Ltd., "Syria: Judiciary," available at: http://www.infoprod.co.il/country/syria2a.htm.

- The jurisdiction of the Courts for Minor Offendors applies accordingly to matters relating to minors.

- The Administrative Courts adjudicate matters involving the state and its agencies.[7]

2. Religious Courts

Because personal status matters are handled by the religious courts, the Syrian government requires each citizen to be affiliated with Christianity, Judaism or Islam. Shari'a courts are the authoritative bodies for Sunni and Shi'a Muslims; the *Madhhabi* Courts are the bodies for Druze; and the *Ruhi* Courts are for Christians and Jews.

3. Recognition of Foreign Judgments

Foreign judgments can only be executed in Syria if they relate to civil or to commercial disputes with the approval of the Court of First Instance in the governorate where the judgment is to be executed. In the absence of a bilateral treaty on mutual recognition with the country concerned, Syrian courts will re-examine the case and the foreign court's opinion before determining whether it will recognize the judgment. If a bilateral treaty exists, the

---

[7] *Id.*

Court will limit its scrutiny to violations of Syrian public policy.[8]

4. Alternative Dispute Resolution

Public or government institutions cannot agree to submit to arbitration in Syria unless provided for by statute and the state can only agree to arbitration if it is bound by treaty. International arbitration held in Syria is subject to Syrian law and is generally covered by the same rules governing domestic arbitration.

Syria is a contracting party to the New York Convention on the Recognition and Enforcement of Foreign Arbitral Awards, yet few investment-state disputes have occurred in Syria during the past several years. Such disputes are usually settled through negotiations or by enforcement of a contractual arbitration clause.[9] When international arbitration does occur, the enforcement of arbitration awards generally follows the same rules as the enforcement of foreign court decisions in Syria.

---

[8] *Id.*

[9] *Id.*

CHAPTER II. PERSONAL STATUS LAWS IN SYRIA

A. OVERVIEW

Like many of the civil legal systems of Europe, which distinguish between the legal status of a person in the public and private spheres, the Syrian judicial system distinguishes between those matters regulated by civil law versus those regulated by personal status law. Personal status law governs a person's relationship within the family sphere as a kinship system, whereas civil law governs a person's rights and obligations with regards to civil society. The delineation between the person's legal status, in both public and private spheres, was codified after Syrian independence and resulted in the formation of the Syrian Personal Status Law, which was issued under Legislative Decree Number 59 for the year 1953 and amended by Law Number /34/ for the year 1975.[10]

The Syrian Personal Status Law (SPSL) affects many aspects of the lives of citizens who choose to settle in Syria or reside here with their families. It is divided into six books, which govern the following issues in Syrian law:

- Book the First: Marriage (الزواج)

---

[10] Unclassified Damascus Briefing 00000657, VZCZCXYZ0000, RR RUEHWEB. FM American Embassy Damascus. E.O. 13526.

- Book the Second: Marital Dissolution (انحلال الزواج)

- Book the Third: Birth and Its Consequences (الولادة
  ونتائجها)

- Book the Fourth: Capacity and Legal Guardianship
  (الأهلية والنيابة الشرعية)

- Book the Fifth: Wills (الوصية)

- Book the Sixth: Inheritance (المواريث)

In addition, the SPSL governs parental rights, determines how citizenship is transmitted, establishes the requirements for marriage and divorce and creates the framework for inheritance. The SPSL places personal status firmly within the governance of recognized religious communities and codifies the practices of the various communities. While the SPSL incorporates elements of gender equity, it also differentiates between the genders, generally providing the more authoritative role to a man. In areas where the SPSL attempts to advance the interests of women, a contrasting male-centric cultural norm often prevails in practice. Cultural norms have also governed attitudes towards domestic violence. However, shelters and hotlines are now being introduced in Syria.[11]

---

[11] *Id.*

SPSL applies to all Syrian citizens regardless of religious denomination, with the exception that non-Muslim religious groups are granted an exemption from that law in matters of marriage, divorce, and, under President Bashar Al-Assad's decree number 76 dated Sep. 26, 2010 to amend article 308 of the code of the Code of Personal Status, inheritance as well.[12] Guardianship and kinship continue to be regulated by the Islamic-influenced SPSL for all Syrians.

In 2006, significant changes were instituted to Catholic family law that gave increased autonomy to the following groups: Roman Catholics, Armenian Catholics, Syrian Catholics, Maronites, Chaldeans, and Latin Catholics in the areas governed by the SPSL. The most important amendments to Catholic family law applied to matters of divorce, inheritance, guardianship, adoption and custody.[13]

---

[12] أصدر الرئيس بشار الأسد المرسوم رقم (76) تاريخ 2010/9/26 قضي بتعديل المادة 308 من قانون الأحوال الشخصية النافذ حالياً والمتعلقة بالطوائف المسيحية واليهودية.

[13] Unclassified Damascus Briefing 00000657, VZCZCXYZ0000, RR RUEHWEB. FM American Embassy Damascus. E.O. 13526.

B. MARRIAGE

1. Overview: Marriage in Practice in Syria

Under Islamic law, marriage is achieved from the moment two individuals holding capacity and in the presence of two witnesses exchange promises vowing to wed one another. In Syria, in order for the state to recognize the marriage and confer on the parties the rights and duties associated with married couples, the marriage must be registered. Most often, a religious court will send a delegate to the home of the couple as a witness (in addition to the two witnesses prescribed in Islam) to the exchange of the vows and signing of a marriage contract. The delegate has the couple sign a marriage registry and then returns to the religious court to register the marriage. Some couples go directly to the religious court to exchange vows, sign a marriage contract and the marriage registry and other couples may exchange vows in the home without a religious court delegate and then at a later time go to the religious court to register the marriage retroactively. After a marriage is registered in the applicable religious court, the religious court sends the contract and registry to the Civil Department to be recorded in each spouse's civil record.[14]

---

[14] Interview with Souhail Abou-Rass, attorney in private practice in Damascus, Syria. 11 November 2010.

In Syria, couples in practice sometimes consider the exchange of vows and the signing of a marriage contract as a mere exchange of promises to live together as husband and wife at some distant time in the future. They consider themselves merely engaged until an agreed upon time in the future where a marriage celebration will be held and it will be publicly proclaimed that they are husband and wife, at which point they begin living together. Regardless of what they believe in practice, the state recognizes the marriage from the date that the vows were exchanged, even if the couple registers the marriage at a later date (retroactive civil recognition of marriage is applicable). In practice, this means that a couple that exchanges vows and follows the legally prescribed procedures for marriage (the presence of witnesses, signing of a marriage contract, and registration in the court) will be considered married by the state and should the couple wish to celebrate before the wedding separation that they consider to be the final seal on their marriage, they must follow all of the legally prescribed procedures outlined in the SPSL for obtaining divorce, as any other married couple. However, if they fail to complete the administrative procedure of registering the marriage in the religious court holding jurisdiction, then they will be viewed by the state as merely engaged, and none of the legal rights and obligations applying to married couples will be applied by the state. They would be free to separate.

There is also an institution formally known as "engagement" (خطبة) in Syria. Unlike the exchange of vows in the religious courts or outside of the courts in the presence of two witnesses, the engagement does not change the couples' legal status under Islam or under the SPSL, does not have any required legal elements, and is not regulated by the law. It consists merely in the couple's mutual exchange of promises to marry one another. Not until the vows are exchanged in the presence of witnesses with the exchange of consideration and the fulfillment of the other legal elements will the marriage be recognized by Islam, and not until this marriage is registered with the applicable religious court and cross-registered with the civil division will the marriage be recognized by the state. Until full legal recognition of the marriage, the wife will not be entitled to her right to alimony, inheritance, or the other protections offered in the SPSL.[15]

The final stage in the consummation of the marital relationship is known as *dakhoul* (دخول), or penetration (sexual consummation of the marriage). It introduces a series of new rights and obligations with respect to

---

[15] *Id.*

revocable and irrevocable divorce, which we examine below.

2. Marriage under the Syrian Personal Status Law

a. *Marriage Contract Elements and Conditions*

The SPSL sets out the elements and conditions required for a valid marriage. It regulates marriage and engagement (الزواج والخطبة), the marriage contract and its elements (أركان العقد وشرائطه), the types of marriage and their provisions (أنواع الزواج وأحكامه), and the effects of marriage (آثار الزواج), which include the dowry, the marital home, and expenses.

The SPSL defines marriage as a "contract between a man and a woman that can be legally consummated in the aim of establishing a common relationship and procreation" (art. 1 SPSL).[16] It is contracted with the consent of one party and the acceptance of the other (art. 5 SPSL).[17] As such, marriage forms a contract that, like any other, must fulfill certain elements in order to be held valid. Among these elements are as follow:

---

[16] الزواج عقد بين رجل وامرأة تحل له شرعاً غايته إنشاء رابطة للحياة المشتركة والنسل (المادة 1).

[17] ـ ينعقد الزواج بإيجاب من أحد العاقدين وقبول من الآخر (المادة 5).

25

a) *Mutual Consent.* A valid offer must be made by the offeror to the offeree, who must accept the offer in terms identical to those in the offer. The two parties must come to a "meeting of the minds."

b) *Contractual Capacity.* The parties must be legally and mentally competent to undertake decisions bearing legal consequences. If the woman is a virgin and it is her first marriage, she needs the approval of her legal guardian (father, grandfather, uncle, brother, or, if none are living or available, by the religious judge).

c) *Consideration.* Consideration is the concept of legal value in connection with a contract. In order for a contract to be enforceable, each party must exchange consideration to the other. In the case of the Syrian marriage contract, the contractual consideration is the promises exchanged by each party to wed the other.

d) *Legality of Purpose.* The contract must not have an illegal object (*e.g.*, marrying in order to commit a fraud). Such contracts are null and void.

e) *Proper Form.* Certain contracts must be ratified by some agencies or authorities; others must only be in writing.

The marital administrative procedures require the parties to present the marriage petition to the Judge of the district with the following documents:

a) A statement from the district's *mokhtar* (مختار: mayor of the district) with the name of the fiancé or fiancée, his/her age, his/her residence, the name of his/her guardian and a certification of no legal objections to this marriage;

b) A certified copy of their Syrian Civil extracts and their personal status;

c) A report from a doctor stating that the parties are free from any contagious diseases or any other medical condition to prevent such marriage. The applicants may choose their own doctor, but the judge may test this matter by choosing another physician;

d) A marriage license for military personnel and for those who are within the compulsory military service age; and

e) Permission from the Immigration Department if one of the parties is a foreigner (art. 40.1 SPSL).[18]

If the judge has any doubts as to the validity of any of the documents presented by the parties, he has the right to

---

[18] يقدم طلب الزواج لقاضي المنطقة مع الوثائق الآتية :

أ ـ شهادة من مختار وعرفاء المحلة باسم كل من الخاطب والمخطوبة وسنة ومحل إقامته واسم وليه وأنه لا يمنع من هذا الزواج مانع شرعي

ب ـ صورة مصدقة عن قيد نفوس الطرفين وأحوالهما الشخصية

ج ـ شهادة من طبيب يختاره الطرفان بخلوهما من الأمراض السارية ومن الموانع الصحية للزواج، وللقاضي التثبت من ذلك بمعرفة طبيب يختاره

د ـ رخصة بالزواج للعسكريين ولمن هم في سن الجندية الإجبارية

هـ ـ موافقة مديرية الأمن العام إن كان أحد الزوجين أجنبياً (المادة 40.1).

delay the declaration of marriage for a period of up to ten days (art. 41 SPSL).[19]

Marriage taking place outside the Court without following the proper procedures is generally not permitted in Syria. However, there are ways to obtain legal recognition of such marriages. For example, if a child was born or a pregnancy occurred, the marriage will be permitted without the above-outlined procedures, but legal penalties will apply (art. 40.2 SPSL).[20] In the absence of a birth or pregnancy, it still may be possible to obtain a "judicial marriage," a marriage established by a legal sentence declaring the marriage to exist, rather than through the signing of a marriage contract in the religious court. This is the course of action taken by many couples who are unable to meet the required elements for a valid marriage under the SPSL. For example, if a couple got married outside of the religious court because they were unable to obtain the certification of a *mokhtar* of no legal objections to the marriage (*e.g.*, the bride's father objected to the marriage), they may nonetheless obtain legal

---

19 يأذن القاضي بإجراء العقد فوراً بعد استكمال هذه الوثائق وله عند الاشتباه تأخيره لإعلانه مدة عشرة أيام والقاضي يختار طريقة الإعلان (المادة 41).

20 لا يجوز تثبيت الزواج المعقود خارج المحكمة إلا بعد استيفاء هذه الإجراءات على أنه إذا حصل ولد أو حمل ظاهر يثبت الزواج بدون هذه الإجراءات ولا يمنع ذلك من إيقاع العقوبة القانونية (المادة 40.2).

recognition of the marriage by petitioning the courts and adjudicating the issue as a normal legal action.[21] Once they obtain a legal sentence retroactively proclaiming the marriage to exist, it will be the sentence rather than a marriage contract that is registered in the civil registry.[22]

b. Marriage Contracts and Execution

After all of these documents are presented, the district Judge may execute the marriage contract immediately. The marriage contract must include the following information:

a) Full name and place of residence of both parties;

b) The date and place of the contract;

c) The name and the place of residence of the witnesses or guardians;

d) The amount of the advanced and postponed dowry, as well as a statement as to whether the advanced dowry was received;

e) The signatures of the parties, the Maazoun (المأذون: the official delegate authorized to execute the

---

[21] Interview with Yamman Samman, attorney in private practice in Damascus, Syria. 10 November 2010.

[22] N.B.: this form of judicial marriage will only be permitted when an insubstantial flaw presents itself in the marriage (e.g., a procedural flaw). If a material flaw presents itself (e.g., a Muslim woman marries an atheist or a follower of a non-Abrahamic or polytheistic faith), then the marriage will be held absolutely void and neither a judge nor a civil registry will recognize the marriage as such. Interview with Souhail Abou-Rass, attorney in private practice in Damascus, Syria. 11 November 2010.

marriage), and the Judge's notarization (art. 44 SPSL).[23]

The Judge or any authorized Court assistant may execute the marriage contract (art. 43 SPSL).[24] If the contract is not executed within six months, the marriage permit expires (art. 42 SPSL).[25]

After the marriage contract is executed, the Court assistant registers the marriage in his special book and sends a copy to the Civil Department (Department of Civil Status) within ten days of the date of the marriage. In this way, the Civil Registry of both parties is automatically updated, reflecting the new personal status of the parties, without the need of either party to inform the Civil Department of the marriage. Failure to register the

---

[23] يجب أن يشمل صك الزواج :

أ ـ أسماء الطرفين كاملة وموطن كل منهما

ب ـ وقوع العقد وتاريخه ومكانه

ج ـ أسماء الشهود والوكلاء كاملة وموطن كل منهم

د ـ مقدار المهر المعجل والمؤجل وهل قبض المعجل أم لا

هـ ـ توقيع أصحاب العلاقة والمأذون وتصديق القاضي (المادة 44).

[24] يقوم القاضي أو من يأذن له من مساعدي المحكمة بإجراء العقد (المادة 43).

[25] إذا لم يجر العقد خلال ستة أشهر يعتبر الإذن ملغى (المادة 42).

marriage in the Civil Department is the responsibility of the Court assistant (art. 45 SPSL).[26]

The same procedure for confirming marriage is followed for registering divorce and death: the Civil Records bookkeeper will register the event in the appropriate registry without any other procedure (art. 45 SPSL).[27] The marriage contract is fee exempted (art. 46 SPSL).[28]

26- 1 يسجل المساعد الزواج في سجله المخصوص ويبعث بصورة عنه لدائرة الأحوال المدنية خلال عشرة أيام من تاريخ الزواج

2- تغني هذه الصورة عن إخبار الطرفين دائرة الأحوال المدنية بالزواج ويكون المساعد مسئولا عن إهمال إرسال الصورة

3- تطبق الطريقة نفسها في تسجيل الأحكام الصادرة بتثبيت الزواج والطلاق والنسب ووفاة المفقود، ويقوم أمين السجل المدني بتدوين ذلك في السجلات

المخصوصة دون حاجة إلى أي إجراء آخر (المادة 45).

27- 1 يسجل المساعد الزواج في سجله المخصوص ويبعث بصورة عنه لدائرة الأحوال المدنية خلال عشرة أيام من تاريخ الزواج

2- تغني هذه الصورة عن إخبار الطرفين دائرة الأحوال المدنية بالزواج ويكون المساعد مسئولا عن إهمال إرسال الصورة

3- تطبق الطريقة نفسها في تسجيل الأحكام الصادرة بتثبيت الزواج والطلاق والنسب ووفاة المفقود، ويقوم أمين السجل المدني بتدوين ذلك في السجلات

المخصوصة دون حاجة إلى أي إجراء آخر (المادة 45).

28 تعفى معاملات الزواج من كل رسم (المادة 46).

3. Recognition of Marriage Abroad and Public Policy Considerations

Syria permits the registration in the Civil Registry of marriages of Syrian citizens abroad. The citizens may register the marriage at the Syrian Embassy in the country in which they are residing or in the Civil Department of Syria. The Syrian authorities will generally grant the marriage full faith and credit, unless it contravenes Syrian public policy. Because Syrian public policy is largely based on Islamic law and jurisprudence, a marriage realized abroad that contravenes these precepts will not be held to be valid under Syrian law.

As a general rule, it can be said that if a marriage would not have been permitted under Syrian law, then it would not be recognized by Syria if it was executed abroad. For example, because Islamic law prohibits a Muslim woman from marrying a Christian man, the Syrian courts will not recognize or register the marriage abroad of a Syrian Muslim woman to a Christian.[29]

---

[29] Interview with Yamman Samman, attorney in private practice in Damascus, Syria. 10 November 2010.

C. MARITAL DISSOLUTION

1. Overview

Marital dissolution is discussed in the Book the Second of the SPSL, articles 85-127, which deal with revocable divorce (الطلاق), dissolution by mutual assent (مخالعة), separation by the court (التفريق) (including separation with cause, due to absence, irreconcilable differences, and abuse), and the consequences of divorce, including the waiting period (العدة).

2. Modes of Divorce

a. Divorce (talaq: الطلاق)

i. Overview

Talaq (الطلاق), the Islamic term for "divorce," is used to end a marriage under the terms of Shari'a. There are differing interpretations as to how divorce is to be effected in practice. In some interpretations, a husband may end a relationship by stating three times "I divorce you," with no witnesses present. Shi'a scholars view the triple *talaq* as *haraam* and forbidden by Muhammad. Some Sunni scholars consider the triple *talaq* as invalid unless each *talaq* was invoked in a different sitting and after the parties have attempted to reconcile with one another. In Syria, the general practice is to pronounce the *talaq* on three different occasions, though stating it once and following through

33

the judicial procedures will sever the marital ties on its own if there is no reconciliation or revocation of the divorce by the husband. The triple *talaq* remains a controversial practice that we examine below.

Under the SPSL, a man has capacity to divorce at the age of eighteen, but a judge may authorize and legalize a divorce before that age if he finds a compelling interest in doing so (art. 85 SPSL).[30] Divorce may be realized either orally or in writing, and the man may divorce his wife himself or authorize another person to divorce on his behalf or authorize the woman to divorce (art. 87 SPSL).[31]

ii. Stages

Talaq under Syrian law involves three stages:

a) First *talaq*. The husband pronounces the *talaq* (أنتِ طالق: "I divorce you"). A divorce application is then presented to the court.

b) Second *talaq*. Waiting period. The judge will postpone the divorce for one month, giving the parties the opportunity for reconciliation.

---

[30] يكون الرجل متمتعاً بالأهلية الكاملة للطلاق في تمام الثامنة عشرة من عمره. يجوز للقاضي أن يأذن بالتطليق، أو يجيز الطلاق الواقع من البالغ المتزوج قبل الثامنة عشرة إذا وجدت المصلحة في ذلك (المادة 85).

[31] 1- يقع الطلاق باللفظ وبالكتابة، ويقع من العاجز عنهما بإشارته المعلومة.2- للزوج أن يوكل غيره بالتطليق وأن يفوض المرأة بتطليق نفسها (المادة 87).

c) Third *talaq*. If, after of the expiration period, the husband or both parties insist on divorce, the judge will call the two parties and listen to their dispute and will seek to resolve it and have them live together. This is known as the تدخل القاضي (entry of the judge), where the judge seeks help from the relatives of both parties and others who are able to resolve the dispute (see art. 88 SPSL).[32]

If the judge's efforts to reconcile the pair fail, he will allow the registration of divorce, which will be retroactively considered effective from the date the husband registered the first *talaq* (art. 88.3 SPSL).[33]

iii. The Dowry and the Sexual Consummation of the Marriage

As mentioned earlier, the final stage in the consummation of the marital relationship is known as the *dakhoul* (دخول), or penetration (sexual consummation of the marriage). If the husband pronounces divorce prior to the

---

[32] -1 : إذا قدمت للمحكمة معاملة طلاق أو معاملة مخالعة أجلها القاضي شهراً أملاً بالصلح

2-إذا أصر الزوج بعد انقضاء المهلة على الطلاق أو أصر الطرفان على المخالعة دعا القاضي الطرفين واستمع إلى خلافهما وسعى إلى إزالته ودوام الحياة الزوجية واستعان على ذلك بمن يراهم من أهل الزوجين وغيرهم ممن يقدرون على إزالة الخلاف (المادة 88.1-2).

[33] وإذا لم تفلح هذه المساعي سمح القاضي بتسجيل الطلاق أو المخالعة واعتبر الطلاق نافذاً من تاريخ إيقاعه (المادة 88,3).

consummation and the wife is thus still a virgin, the wife is entitled to only half of her dowry. If the marriage has been consummated sexually, the wife may keep the dowry (مهر). If at their marriage, the husband only paid half of the dowry,[34] she has the right to demand payment of the second half. In addition, she is entitled to all of the personalty in the home.

iv. Revocable and Irrevocable *Talaq*

After the husband pronounces the *talaq* the first time, he may revoke the divorce and take his wife back within a period of three months. Thus, if after the application for divorce is filed and the one month waiting period expires, neither of the parties follow up over a period of three months starting from the date of the application, it will be presumed that the husband revoked the divorce and the divorce application will be deleted (art. 88.4 SPSL).[35] However, if his wife is a virgin, then the couple can only be reconciled if a new marital contract is formed.

After the husband pronounces the second *talaq*, he may once again take the wife back within a period of three months. If, however, he pronounces the *talaq* a third time,

---

[34] This custom allows men who otherwise would be unable to pay the entire dowry at once at marriage to pay the dowry.

[35] تشطب المعاملة بمرور ثلاثة أشهر اعتباراً من تاريخ الطلب إذا لم يراجع بشأنها أي من الطرفين (المادة 88.4).

then the divorce is irrevocable and the only way to take the wife back would be to have her first marry another man, consummate the marriage, obtain a divorce, and, after the *iddah* (*see infra.*), remarry the original husband with a new marriage contract.[36]

In this spirit, the SPSL states that each divorce can be revoked except for that of the virgin wife [requires a new contract] and that of the third *talaq* [requires a new contract and marriage to another man] (art. 94 SPSL).[37] Thus, when the SPSL states that a husband has the right to divorce three times (art. 91 SPSL),[38] it is referring to the right of the husband to divorce his wife three times before it becomes irrevocable and he can no longer divorce her, unless she marries another man, obtains a divorce, and then marries the first man. It is not referring to a man's right to obtain divorces with different women; the man may marry and divorce as many different women as he pleases. Rather, he is limited in the number of times that he may divorce any single wife before the divorce becomes irrevocable.

---

[36] Interview with Daad Mousa, attorney in private practice in Damascus, Syria. 14 November 2010.

[37] ـ كل طلاق يقع رجعياً إلا المكمل للثلاث والطلاق قبل الدخول، والطلاق على بدل وما نص على كونه بائناً في هذا القانون (المادة 94).

[38] ـ يملك الزوج على زوجته ثلاث طلقات (المادة 91).

v. Relationship of the Spouses during *Talaq*

When the husband pronounces *talaq*, the marital relationship is ruptured, unless and until the husband revokes the *talaq*. During the time in which the relationship is ruptured, the woman may continue to live in the home, but she becomes estranged from the husband and must treat him as a stranger. If she is accustomed to the *hijab*, she will wear it in his presence. Sexual intercourse between the couple during this time would be the equivalent of adultery under Islamic law.[39]

vi. The Triple *Talaq*

Article 92 SPSL states that the *talaq* joined together by a word (*e.g.*, "I divorce you in three": أنتِ طالق بالثلاث) or by a sign (*e.g.*, stating the *talaq* while holding up three fingers) counts only as one *talaq*.[40] Some attorneys have narrowly interpreted the article to mean that to achieve irrevocable divorce in Syria through a triple *talaq* in one sitting, all three pronunciations of the *talaq* must be stated separately (*i.e.*, the husband must pronounce "I divorce you, I divorce you, I divorce you" rather than "I divorce you in three." They hold that three individual pronunciations of *talaq* in

---

[39] Interview with Souhail Abou-Rass, attorney in private practice in Damascus, Syria. 11 November 2010.

[40] ـ الطلاق المقترن بعدد لفظاً أو إشارة لا يقع إلا واحداً (المادة 92).

one sitting will have the effect of achieving irrevocable divorce, such that the judicial adjudication of divorce does not require the entry of the judge to attempt to reconcile the couple, since the divorce is final.

Other attorneys have read the article as restricting the effect of the triple *talaq* pronounced in one sitting in any context, whether stated as "I divorce you in three" or as three separate pronunciations of "I divorce you." They hold that the triple *talaq* is irrelevant to the Syrian judicial proceeding because once the triple *talaq* is pronounced, the couple will be considered estranged under Islamic law, and therefore, the Syrian judicial proceeding for divorce, which is intended for married couples, cannot be utilized. Therefore, in Syria, the triple *talaq* serves as a single *talaq* that must be adjudicated according to the legal procedures prescribed in the SPSL.[41]

vii. Limits to *Talaq*

The *talaq* is not recognized if it occurred when the husband's will and awareness were somehow compromised by circumstances that negate his capacity to make a rational decision. It will thus not be recognized when the husband was drunk, provoked, in the heat of passion, or under any other undue influences (see art. 89

---

[41] Interview with Yamman Samman, attorney in private practice in Damascus, Syria. 10 November 2010.

SPSL).[42] The declaration of the *talaq* is considered invalid if used as a means of coercion, duress, or other undue influence or if invoked in swearing (affirming) (art. 90 SPSL).[43] However, the SPSL at the same time states that intention is not a necessary element when the words of the *talaq* are clearly pronounced. The divorce also occurs with the declaration of synonym expressions that hold the meaning of divorce (art. 93 SPSL).[44]

viii.   The Woman's Right to *Talaq*

The default provision in Syria is that the *talaq* is the right of the man only. However, women may obtain *talaq* if they reserve their right to do so in the "Special Provisions" (شروط خاصة) section of the marriage contract. This section is normally left blank, but the couple may include therein any provisions to which they both agree and which are not against public policy. Thus, in a sense, a woman may obtain *talaq*; but in another sense, she is not doing so unilaterally because the husband is consenting to these

---

[42] -1 :- لا يقع طلاق السكران ولا المدهوش ولا المكره

2- المدهوش هو الذي فقد تمييزه من غضب أو غيره فلا يدري ما يقول (المادة 89).

[43] - لا يقع الطلاق غير المنجز إذا لم يقصد به إلا الحث على فعل شيء أو المنع منه أو استعمل استعمال القسم لتأكيد الإخبار لا غير (المادة 90).

[44] - يقع الطلاق بالألفاظ الصريحة فيه عرفاً دون حاجة إلى نية، ويقع بالألفاظ الكنائية التي تحتمل معنى الطلاق وغيره بالنية (المادة 93).

terms in the marriage contract. For the man, even if the right to a obtain a *talaq* is not included in the marriage contract, he may obtain one through the provisions established in the SPSL.[45]

b. Dissolution by Mutual Assent (mukhul'a: مخالعة)

i. Mukhul'a as an Islamic Institution

Some Sunni schools of jurisprudence allow women to petition for a divorce under certain conditions. Such a divorce is known as *mukhul'a* (مخالعة). The term *mukhul'a* comes from the root *mukhul'a* (خلع), which means to separate or remove.

Unlike the *talaq*, where the woman has the right to keep the dowry and marital personalty, the terms of the divorce in the *mukhul'a* are determined according to the mutual assent of the parties. There must, however, be some contractual consideration (البدل) in order for the contract to be valid (art. 98 SPSL).[46] The consideration could be anything from all of the marital property to nominal consideration, such as five hundred Syrian pounds (US $10), that serve nothing as more than a mere

---

[45] Interview with Yamman Samman, attorney in private practice in Damascus, Syria. 10 November 2010.

[46] ـ إذا كانت المخالعة على مال غير المهر لزم أداؤه وبرئت ذمة المتخالعين من كل حق يتعلق بالمهر والنفقة الزوجية (المادة 98).

formality. In practice, the consideration will be a nominal amount given by the wife to the husband in exchange for her freedom. Because it is a mere formality, the consideration is not usually paid. The *mukhul'a* thus allows the wife to obtain a divorce more rapidly than would otherwise be possible in the drawn out process inherent to the *talaq*. However, the wife must be open to giving up her right to keep the dowry and marital property, if those are the terms that the husband demands in order to agree to the *mukhul'a*.

The institution of the *mukhul'a* is based in *Aya* 2:229 of the Qur'an, which states: "It is not lawful for you, [Men], to take back any of your gifts [from your wives], except when both parties fear that they would be unable to keep the limits ordained by Allah. If ye [judges] do indeed fear that they would be unable to keep the limits ordained by Allah, there is no blame on either of them if she give something [the *mahr*] for her freedom [*mukhul'a*]."[47] This has been understood to mean that if the wife seeks a divorce, and she is willing to give up her dowry, then she may with the assent of the husband obtain the divorce by returning the dowry. However, as stated earlier, the practice has evolved to allow the couple the discretion to

---

[47] *The Holy Quran, English Translation of the Meanings by Abdullah Yusuf Ali:* Baqara 2:229.

agree that the wife keep the dowry or other marital property.

ii. Regulation under Syrian Law

In Syria, the *mukhul'a* is governed by articles 95 to 104 of the SPSL. Considered to be divorce by mutual assent (art. 96 SPSL),[48] the contract of the *mukhul'a* requires the fulfillment of the same elements as the marital contract, namely: mutual acceptance, contractual capacity, valid consideration, legality of purpose, and proper form (see arts. 95 *et seqq.* SPSL).[49] If the contract lacks any of these elements, then it will not be considered a divorce by mutual assent, but rather, a revocable divorce (الطلاق) whereby the husband may reinstitute the marriage within the allowable period without the need for establishing a new marital contract (art. 100 SPSL).[50] Because the terms of the contract are to be established by the assent of the parties, they may agree that the husband will be released from the obligation to pay alimony, if such is explicitly

---

[48] ـ لكل من الطرفين الزوجون عن إيجابه في المخالعة قبل قبول الآخر(المادة 96).

[49] ـ: 1ـ يشترط لصحة المخالعة أن يكون الزوج أهلاً لإيقاع الطلاق والمرآة محلاً له. ـ2 المرآة التي لم تبلغ سن الرشد إذا خولعت لا تلتزم ببدل الخلع إلا بموافقة ولي المال (المادة 95).

[50] ـ إذا صرح المتخالعان بنفي البدل كانت المخالعة في حكم الطلاق المحض ووقع بها طلقة رجعية (المادة 100).

mentioned in the contract of (art. 101 SPSL).[51] However, certain provisions, if against public policy, will be held void, while the rest of the contract will stand. For example, if the husband has stipulated in the contract that the child's custody should be given to him, then this clause will be struck from the contract (art. 103 SPSL).[52]

Divorce through the *mukhul'a* in Syria becomes effective from the date that the parties came to agree to the *mukhul'a*.

c. Separation by the Court (tafreeq: التفريق)

If any party to the marriage has failed to meet his or her obligations under the marriage contract or has mistreated the other party, then the injured party can petition the judge to end the marriage by declaring the separation of the spouses. Thus, unlike *talaq*, which can only be initiated through the will of the husband, the *tafreeq* permits the wife to initiate a divorce proceeding in the courts. However, unlike the no-fault based system of *talaq* where the husband may obtain a divorce without showing cause, the *tafreeq* can only be achieved if the

[51] ـ نفقة العدة لا تسقط ولا يبرأ الزوج المخالع منها إلا إذا نص عليها صراحة في عقد المخالعة (المادة 101).

[52] ـ إذا اشترط الرجل في المخالعة إمساك الولد عنده مدة الحضانة صحت المخالعة وبطل الشرط وكان لحاضنته الشرعية أخذه منه ويلزم أبوه بنفقته. وأجرة حضانته إن كان الولد فقيراً (المادة 103).

petitioner meets a burden of proving the existence of one of the enumerated causes, which we examine below.

Wives will choose to adjudicate a divorce via *tafreeq* because the *talaq* is available only to husbands. Husbands may choose to adjudicate a divorce via *tafreeq* in order to avoid having to pay the wife alimony, permitting the wife to keep the entire dowry, or to avoid the other financial consequences of *talaq*. In *tafreeq*, these consequences are largely determined by the circumstances and the mediator.[53]

Unlike *talaq*, which is recognized retroactively from the date that the husband first registered the divorce, the *tafreeq* is recognized from the date in which the judge gives the order.

i.   Separation with Cause (arts. 105-108 SPSL)

The woman may petition for divorce if the man is sexually impotent However, if the wife is infertile, she may not petition for divorce on this basis. Similarly, if the man becomes insane, the wife may petition for divorce (art. 105 SPSL).[54] However, if the woman, prior to the marriage, is

---

[53] Interview with Daad Mousa, attorney in private practice in Damascus, Syria. 14 November 2010.

[54] ـ للزوجة طلب التفريق بينها وبين زوجها في الحالتين التاليتين :

1ـ إذا كان فيه إحدى العلل المانعة من الدخول بشرط سلامتها هي منها

aware of a cause of illness that may lead to the voidance of the marriage, then she may not petition for the divorce on this basis. If, however, the cause of divorce is the husband's impotence, the petition can be made regardless of whether the wife had foreknowledge (art. 106 SPSL).[55] As a defense, the husband may show within one year that the illness is curable and he has up to one year to do so. This defense is at the discretion of the judge (art. 107 SPSL).[56] Furthermore, the wife may obtain *tafreeq* is she swears to the judge that the husband divorced her three times (pronounced three *talaqs*) (art. 108 SPSL).[57]

ii. Separation due to Absence (art. 109 SPSL)

If the man leaves the home and does not return and the wife does not know where he is, then after a one year

---

2-إذا جن الزوج بعد العقد (المادة 105).

[55] -: 1- يسقط حق المرأة في طلب التفريق بسبب العلل المبينة في المادة السابقة إذا علمت بها قبل العقد أو رضيت بها بعده

2-على أن حق التفريق بسبب العنة لا يسقط بحال (المادة 106).

[56] - إذا كانت العلل المذكورة في المادة 105 غير قابلة الزوال يفرق القاضي بين الزوجين في الحال وإن كان زوالها ممكناً يؤجل الدعوى مدة مناسبة

لا تتجاوز السنة فإذا لم تزل العلة فرق بينهما (المادة 107).

[57] - التفريق للعلة طلاق بائن (المادة 108).

waiting period, the wife may institute a divorce proceeding (art. 109 SPSL).[58]

iii. Separation due to Constructive Abandonment (arts. 110-111 SPSL)

If because of the marriage the wife is prevented from living a decent life because the husband spends no money on her, she can obtain a divorce. However, if the husband becomes aware of the judicial proceeding and intervenes, he may defend against the action if he can prove that he is poor or that he is on leave (*e.g.*, on military service). In such a case, he may have the divorce order vacated (art. 110 SPSL).[59] This divorce is also revocable if, after the judge pronounced the divorce order, the man reforms himself and the wife agrees to remarry) (art. 111 SPSL).[60]

---

[58] -: 1- إذا غاب الزوج بلا عذر مقبول أو حكم بعقوبة السجن أكثر من ثلاث سنوات جاز لزوجته بعد سنة من الغياب أو السجن أن تطلب إلى القاضي التفريق ولو كان له مال تستطيع الإنفاق منه

2-هذا التفريق طلاق رجعي فإذا رجع الغائب أو أطلق السجين والمرآة في العدة حق له مراجعتها (المادة 109).

[59] -: 1- يجوز للزوجة طلب التفريق إذا امتنع الزوج الحاضر عن الإنفاق على زوجته ولم يكن له مال ظاهر ولم يثبت عجزه عن النفقة

2-إن أثبت عجزه أو كان غائباً أمهله القاضي مدة مناسبة لا تتجاوز ثلاثة أشهر فإن لم ينفق فرق القاضي بينهما (المادة 110).

[60] - تفريق القاضي لعدم الإنفاق يقع رجعياً وللزوج أن يراجع زوجته في العدة بشرط أن يثبت يساره ويستعد للإنفاق (المادة 111).

iv. Separation due to Irreconcilable Differences (arts. 112-
115 SPSL).

If one of the parties goes to the court and proves that
the relationship is marked by such irreconcilable
differences that grave and continuous emotional distress
has resulted (*e.g.*, remaining together causes the wife's
depression or other mental illness), then a divorce may be
ordered (art. 112 SPSL).[61] This may be verified by a
judicially-appointed independent source, such as a doctor
(art. 113 SPSL).[62]

---

[61] ـ: 1ـ إذا ادعى أحد الزوجين إضرار الآخر به بما لا يستطاع معه دوام
العشرة يجوز له أن يطلب من القاضي التفريق

2ـإذا ثبت الإضرار وعجز القاضي عن الإصلاح فرق بينهما ويعتبر هذا
التطليق طلقة بائنة

3ـإذا لم يثبت الضرر يؤجل القاضي المحاكمة مدة لا تقل عن شهر أملاً
بالمصالحة فإن أصر المدعي على الشكوى ولم يتم الصلح عين القاضي
حكمين من أهل

الزوجين وإلا ممن يرى القاضي فيه قدرة على الإصلاح بينهما وحلفهما
يميناً على أن يقوما بمهمتهما بعدل و أمانة (المادة 112).

[62] ـ: 1ـ على الحكمين أن يتعرفا أسباب الشقاق بين الزوجين وأن
يجمعاهما في مجلس تحت إشراف القاضي لا يحضره إلا الزوجان ومن
يقرر دعوته
الحكمان

2ـامتناع أحد الزوجين عن حضور هذا المجلس بعد تبليغه لا يؤثر في
التحكيم (المادة 113).

v. Separation due to Abusive *Talaq* (arts. 116-117 SPSL).

If the husband uses the *talaq* in an abusive way (*e.g.*, to threaten or punish his wife or to prevent her from inheriting), the wife may petition for *tafreeq* (art. 116 SPSL).[63] In this case, the judge can order alimony for a period of three years to be paid by the husband either in a lump sum or in monthly payments (art. 117 SPSL).[64, 65]

3. Recognition of Divorce Abroad and Public Policy Considerations

As discussed earlier ("Recognition of Marriage Abroad and Public Policy Considerations," *supra*.), Syria will not recognize marriages abroad that contravene Syrian public

---

[63] ـ من باشر سبباً من أسباب البينونة في مرض موته أو في حالة يغلب في مثلها الهلاك طائعا بلا رضا زوجته ومات في ذلك المرض أو في تلك الحالة والمرآة في العدة فإنها ترث منه بشرط أن تستمر أهليتها للإرث من وقت الإبانة إلى الموت (المادة 116).

[64] ـ إذا طلق الرجل زوجته وتبين للقاضي أن الزوج متعسف في طلاقها دون ما سبب معقول وأن الزوجة سيصيبها بذلك بؤس وفاقة جاز للقاضي أن

يحكم لها على مطلقها بحسب حاله ودرجة تعسفه بتعويض لا يتجاوز مبلغ نفقة ثلاث سنوات لأمثالها فوق نفقة العدة، وللقاضي أن يجعل دفع هذا التعويض جملة

أو شهرياً بحسب مقتضى الحال (المادة 117).

[65] Interpretations of the *tafreeq* laws by Souhail Abou-Rass, attorney in private practice in Damascus, Syria, during 11 November 2010 interview.

policy considerations. The legal recognition of the divorce of Syrian citizens is similarly subject to these public policy considerations. Because the default rule in Syria is that only the man may obtain *talaq* (unilateral divorce), then a woman who goes abroad to obtain a divorce will be unable to register the divorce if she does not have the husband's consent, unless the spouses agreed to grant her this right in the marriage contract. Furthermore, if the woman is a Muslim, then the divorce will not be recognized if she obtained it from a secular civil authority abroad, since Syrian policy requires Muslims to submit to the jurisdiction of the religious (Shar'ia) courts. She would have a better chance of receiving Syrian recognition and registration of the divorce if it were authorized by a Muslim religious authority.[66]

4. Waiting Period Prior to Remarriage (العدة)

In Islam, the "iddah" (العدة) is the period a woman must wait after the death of her spouse or after a divorce, during which she may not marry another man. The *iddah* was intended to make known whether a woman was pregnant with the offspring of her former husband. In Syria, the regulations concerning the *iddah* are governed in articles

---

[66] Interview with Yamman Samman, attorney in private practice in Damascus, Syria. 10 November 2010.

121-127 of the SPSL. The following waiting periods apply in Syria:

- The waiting period for the death of a spouse, as recorded in the Qur'an, is four months and ten days[67, 68]; the waiting period after divorce is three months.
- Non-pregnant women in divorce cases are required to wait three full menstrual cycles. However, if a woman does not menstruate, she must wait three months before she is able to remarry (art. 121.1 SPSL).[69] Thus, if a woman has normal menstrual cycles, the *iddah* is measured according to three cycles; otherwise, it is measured according to three months.
- Three months is imposed because of the anomaly of some women who menstruate only once every 90 days. In order to ascertain that they are truly not pregnant, a full 90 day period is imposed on all women to determine whether a pregnancy is present.
- If a woman is pregnant, she must wait until delivery before remarrying. If she has not yet reached the age of menstruation or reached it but then lost it, because waiting a mere three months

---

[67] *The Holy Quran, English Translation of the Meanings by Abdullah Yusuf Ali:* Baqara 2: 234 – 235.

[68] ‫ـ عدة المتوفى عنها زوجها أربعة أشهر وعشرة أيام (المادة 123).‬

[69] ‫ـ عدة المرآة غير الحامل للطلاق أو الفسخ كما يلي :‬

‫ثلاث حيضات كاملات لمن تحيض ولا تسمع دعوى المرآة بانقضائها قبل مضي ثلاثة أشهر على الطلاق أو الفسخ (المادة 121.1).‬

can indicate either that she is pregnant or that simply not menstruating due to age, a full one year waiting period is imposed in order to be able to determine whether a pregnancy is present (art. 121.2 SPSL).[70]

D. CUSTODIANSHIP, LEGAL GUARDIANSHIP, AND CAPACITY

1. Custodianship

The SPSL bases child custody awards upon standard criteria that differ for boys and girls. SPSL awards custody to the divorced mother for boys under the age of 13, and for girls under the age of 15. After these ages, custody reverts automatically to the father until the child turns 18 or marries, whichever comes first.

2. Legal Guardianship and Capacity

The SPSL also distinguishes between the custodianship and the guardianship of the child. While a divorced mother may be the custodian and therefore responsible for the day-to-day care of young children, the father retains the authoritative role as guardian of the children. As guardian, he has the authority to manage the child's money and directs the child's moral upbringing, with

---

[70] سنة كاملة لممتدة الطهر التي يجيئها الحيض أو جاءها ثم انقطع ولم تبلغ سن اليأس (المادة 121.2).

direct control of matters relating to the child's education, healthcare, career, and marriage choice.[71]

Except for the six Catholic denominations granted an exception in 2006, SPSL for guardianship applies to all Syrians regardless of religious denomination. Guardianship, as with custodianship, ends when a child reaches the age of majority at 18. However male-centric traditions have been known to sidestep national law. The US Embassy in Damascus, for example, has heard of a case where a *sheikh* refused to perform the marriage ceremony of a woman whose father was not present to grant his approval, even though she was a twenty three year old major. Similarly, during a Consular Corps luncheon in early 2010, a well-known human rights lawyer and activist provided examples of instances in which both majors and minors were denied their individual rights, in favor of the will of a male guardian with regards to travel or marriage. This contact gave an example from her work with the German Embassy, where two Kurdish-German girls (both under the age of eighteen) in Qamishili were prevented from departing Syria by their uncle who claimed to be their guardian. They were subsequently forced to remain in Syria and marry their relatives. They appealed in court

---

[71] Unclassified Damascus Briefing 00000657, VZCZCXYZ0000, RR RUEHWEB. FM American Embassy Damascus. E.O. 13526.

and lost. The attorney also described another case where a German-Syrian woman over the age of eighteen was prevented from leaving Syria because her uncle was able to lay claim as her guardian and place a travel hold on her. In this case, because the woman was a major (twenty one years of age), she was able to successfully appeal the travel ban and leave the country. The attorney notes that women under eighteen years of age traveling to Syria should be aware that a Syrian male relative, such as a father, uncle, brother, or cousin, may take the role of their legal guardian and place a travel ban on them.[72]

E. WILLS AND INHERITANCE

Wills (الوصية) and inheritance (الإرث) are respectively covered in Books V and VI of the SPSL (arts. 207 - 308), which have historically applied to all Syrian citizens, regardless of religious denomination. Recently, under President Bashar Al-Assad's decree number 76 dated Sept. 26, 2010 to amend article 308 of the code of the Code of Personal Status, inheritance and wills are now exempted by the largely Islamic-influenced SPSL for certain non-Muslim denominations. Article 308 was previously written to state "It applies in relation to Christian and Jewish communities to whatever each community has of

---

[72] *Id.*

legislative religious provisions related to engagement and marriage conditions and contract, and follow-ups and alimony and minor expenses and the invalidity of marriage, dissolution and dowry and custody" (art. 308 SPSL).73 After the Sept. 26, 2010 amendment, inheritance and wills were added to the list of subjects that would be exempted from the SPSL, thus making matters related to inheritance and wills the specialty of the religious courts. Under the Presidential Decree, all contrary provisions of the law of the Roman Catholic community No. 31, the law of the Roman Orthodox community No. 24, and the Law of the Syriac Orthodox community No. 10 are to be cancelled. The provisions of the SPSL relating to wills and inheritance therefore no longer apply to Christian and Jewish minorities.

---

73 ـ يطبق بالنسبة إلى الطوائف المسيحية واليهودية ما لدى كل طائفة من أحكام تشريعية دينية تتعلق في الخطبة وشروط الزواج وعقده، والمتابعة والنفقة الزوجية ونفقة الصغير وبطلان الزواج وحله وانفكاك رباطه وفي البائنة (الدوطة) والحضانة (المادة 307).

CHAPTER III. ADOPTION

A. ADOPTION AND ISLAM

Adoption as practiced in western countries is not recognized as an institution in Islam, since Islam teaches that the ties between a child and his or her biological parents can never be severed. The notion of adoption, where the adoptive parents undertake all of the rights and obligations of the biological parents, known in Arabic as تبني, is considered *haraam* (forbidden) in Islam. Rather, Islam recognizes the institution of guardianship (ولاية), which permits one to raise and nurture abandoned children, orphans, and other children lacking care and support. Under this institution, guardians do not hold all of the rights of the biological parents. For example, should the biological parents ever appear, they would have the right to take custody of their children from the adoptive parents. Furthermore, the adopted children cannot inherit the property of their adopted parents, nor can the adoptive parents inherit the property of the adopted children, as the institution of inheritance is transmitted through blood relationships only.

B. ADOPTION FOR NON-MUSLIMS IN SYRIA: THE CATHOLIC ADOPTION LAW

In Syria, while adoption is not legally recognized as an institution in the SPSL, it is permitted for non-Muslims according to their respective religious codes. Currently, the only religious code in place that allows for adoption is the relatively new Catholic adoption law, contained in Section 5 (arts. 22 – 82) of the Personal Status Law of the Catholic Communities in Syria no. 31 of 2006 (قانون الأحوال الشخصية للطوائف الكاثوليكية في سورية - قانون رقم 31 لعام 2006) (hereinafter, "CPSL"). However, there has been some question as to whether the adoption law is currently valid law, as some attorneys have interpreted the Sept. 26, 2010 Presidential Decree as nullifying the entire CPSL by adding to art. 308 SPSL inheritance and wills as governed by the laws of one's religious community and then cancelling any contrary provisions of the CPSL. One attorney that was interviewed stated that only those provisions of the Catholic adoption law that contradict the Presidential Decree (*i.e.*, any provision that subjects wills and inheritance of adopted children to the Shar'ia rather than to the applicable religious laws) is cancelled by the Presidential Decree, but the rest of the law is valid and remains applicable. In contrast, the attorney Daad Mousa reads the provision of the Presidential Decree that cancels "all contrary provisions of the law of the Roman Catholic community" as holding the entire CPSL to be invalid, and she has cited the voiced disapproval of the Catholic and Christian communities in Syria, as well as the many letters sent to the president protesting this change, as evidence of this view. Under this view, the former Catholic Personal Status Law, which has older and more primitive provisions, has come back into effect as the new CPSL has been repealed.[74] In the event that those provisions of the CPSL that do not contravene the Presidential Decree will continue to apply, or that the CPSL is by another Presidential Decree reinstituted, we continue our previous analysis of adoption under the law.

The CPSL recognizes full and final adoptions as a legal convention and defines the conditions, rights and duties implied therein. In order to adopt an abandoned Syrian child from an orphanage, the following requirements must be met:

a) Proof that the Ministry of Social Affairs recognizes the orphanage.

b) A copy of the police report on how the child was found.

c) Statement from the orphanage about how the child was released to them.

---

[74] Interview with Daad Mousa, attorney in private practice in Damascus, Syria. 14 November 2010.

d) A contract between you and the orphanage showing that they are officially releasing the child to you.

e) Permission from the Syrian Ministry of Social Affairs granting custody of the child to the adopting parents and allowing the adopting parents to travel with the child for immigration.75

However, there have been to date no cases of successful adoption under the still relatively new Catholic adoption law, and one case that has come to the attention of the US Embassy in Damascus has demonstrated that the various ministries in Syria have adopted different and conflicting interpretations of the procedures required for international adoption under the law.

Some attorneys believe that the Catholic Adoption Law will ultimately fail because of public policy considerations: Islam prohibits adoption. Other attorneys believe that these considerations have been adequately dealt with in the law. For example, the orphaned child cannot be a Muslim under the Catholic adoption law, and so it does not affect those who would be governed by Shar'ia and

---

[75] Embassy of the United States in Syria, "Adoption: Information on International Adoptions," available at
http://damascus.usembassy.gov/adoption.html.

other Islamic institutions. Furthermore, the law tries to assure that the adoptive parents and the orphan share the same religion. If the adopted child is Catholic, the parent should be Catholic as well, unless the Catholic authorities allow him to be adopted by a believing Christian from another eastern church (*e.g.*, the Eastern Orthodox Church) (art. 69 CPSL).[76] In any event, leave to adopt is never automatic; the relevant Catholic authorities must first approve the adoption under their discretion.

Similarly, under the adoption law, although the adopted child's name is changed to that of the adopting family, he or she continues to keep many ties with the biological parents, whose relationship is never fully cut off. In a sense, the adopted child remains a member of the original family, though the adoptive family possesses his custody and the obligations associated with his guardianship. While the adoptive parents possess parental rights and obligations towards the adopted child, the adopted child possesses rights and obligations towards his biological parents. In this same manner, if adoptive parents pass away or lose their capacity to raise the child,

---

[76] متبني الكاثوليكي يجب أن يكون كاثوليكياً، ما لم توافق السلطة الكنسية على أن يكون المتبني مؤمناً مسيحياً من إحدى الكنائس الشرقية غير الكاثوليكية. غير أن ذلك لا يستلزم حتماً وحدة الطقس (المادة 69).

guardianship returns to the biological parents (*see* art. 76 CPSL).[77,78]

---

[77] المادّة 76: يبقى المتبنى عضواً في عائلته الأصلية. له فيها كل الحقوق وعليه نحوها جميع الواجبات، على أن حقوقَ السلطة الوالدية عليه تنحصر في متبنيه ما دام هذا حياً وأهلاً لها. أمّا عند وفاته أو فقدانه الأهلية فتعود إلى والد المتبنى أو إلى من يقوم مقامه (المادة 76).

[78] Interview with Yamman Samman, attorney in private practice in Damascus, Syria. 10 November 2010.

APPENDICES

SYRIAN PERSONAL STATUS LAW (EXTRACTS)

Issued under Legislative decree Number 95
for the year 1953
Amended by law number /34/ for the year 1975

English Translation

Book the First. Marriage

Article 1:

Marriage is a contract between a man and a woman that can be legally consummated in the aim of establishing a common relationship and to have children.

Contract elements and conditions - Acceptance and declaration:

Article 5:

The marriage is contracted with the consent of one party and the acceptance of the other.

Marriage administrative procedures:

Procedures prior to the marriage contract:

Article 40:

1. The marriage petition is presented to the Judge of the district with the following documents:

a) Statement from the district's mokhtar (i.e. mayor of the district) with the name of the fiancé or fiancée, his/her age, his/her residence, the name of his/her guardian and a no legal objection to this marriage.

b) Certified copy of their Syrian Civil extract and their personal status

c) A report from the doctor (applicant can choose his own doctor) stating that they are free from any contagious diseases or any other medical objection to prevent such marriage. The judge may ascertain this matter by choosing another physician.

d) A marriage license for military personnel and for those who are within the compulsory military service age

e) Permission from the Immigration Department if one of them is a foreigner

f) It is not allowed to confirm a marriage which took place outside the Court without following these procedures, however, if a child was born or a pregnancy occurred, the marriage will be confirmed without these procedures, with legal penalties.

Article 41:

After the completion of all these documents, the Judge may permit to execute the contract immediately. If the judge has doubts, he has the right to delay it to for declaration for the period of ten days. He has the right to choose the way of declaration.

Article 42:

If the contract is not executed within six month, the marriage permission is cancelled.

Article 43:

The Judge or any authorized Court assistant can execute the marriage contract

Article 44:

The marriage contract should include the following:

a)Full name and place of residence of both parties

b)The date and place of the contract

c)The name and the place of residence of the witnesses or guardians

d)The amount of the advanced and postponed dowry. State if the advanced is received

e)Signatures of parties, the Maazoun (he is the official delegate authorized to execute the marriage) and the Judge notarization.

Article 45:

a)The Court assistant registers the marriage in his special book and sends a copy to the Civil Department within 10 days of the date of the marriage.

b)This copy exempts the couple from informing the Civil Dept of the marriage execution. Failure to do so is the responsibility of the Court assistant.

c)The same procedure are followed for registering issued court orders to confirm the marriage, the divorce, the relationship and the death of a missing person, the Civil Records bookkeeper will register that in the appropriate registry without any other procedure.

Article 46:

Marriage contracts are fee exempted.

Book the Second. Marital Dissolution

Article 95

1. In order to have a valid mukhul'a contract, the husband must be legally competent to divorce his wife.

2. If the wife in a mukhul'a contract is a minor, then the financial reward determined in the contract cannot be binding on her unless it is ratified by her legal guardian [normally her father, grandfather, uncle, etc.]

Article 96

Since the mukhul'a contract should be based on mutual consent, which includes a valid offer and acceptance between the husband and wife, the offer made by either party in order to induce the formation of the contract may be revoked anytime, provided it has not yet been accepted by the other party.

Article 97

The financial reward of the mukhal'a contract can be any asset deemed to be valid consideration in any normal contract.

Article 98

If the financial reward of the mukhal'a contract was not the marriage dowry, then the financial reward must be paid and will release both parties from any and all rights, claims and demands they have or shall have regarding the marriage dowry and alimony.

Article 99

If the parties to the mukhal'a contract have not clearly determined what shall be covered by the financial reward, then this contract will include a general release for any debt, claim or demand they have against one another.

Article 100

If the parties have explicitly declared that there is no financial reward for the mukhal'a contract, then it is not considered as a mukhal'a contract but rather as a revocable divorce. This shall mean that the husband can restore his wife and marriage within the allowed period without the need for a new marriage contract.

Article 101

In the case of divorce, the husband may only be released from the obligation to pay alimony if the same is explicitly stated in the contract.

Article 102

1. If the husband is released from the obligation to pay child support, or it was agreed that child support would be covered by the wife for a certain period, but the wife abandons her child, then the husband shall have the right of reimbursement on what he spends on the child for the remaining period mentioned in the mukhal'a contract.

2. If the wife suffers from financial difficulties, then the husband shall undertake to pay the child support. The amount expended by the husband is considered a debt to be repaid by the wife.

Article 103

If the husband has stipulated in the mukhul'a contract that child custody should be awarded to him, this clause shall be considered void and severed from the remainder of the contract, which shall remain valid. Child custody is to be regulated by mandatory rules of law. The legal guardian appointed by law may obtain custody of the child from the father, thought it shall remain the father's responsibly to pay for child support.

Article 104

If the person awarded child custody was indebted to the child's father, the debt may not be discharged through the payment of child support imposed on the father. The father shall be requested to prove the payment of the child support before claiming payment of such a debt.

الكتاب الاول: الزواج

المادة 1

- الزواج عقد بين رجل وامرأة تحل له شرعاً غايته إنشاء رابطة للحياة المشتركة والنسل

المادة 5

- ينعقد الزواج بإيجاب من أحد العاقدين وقبول من الآخر

المادة 40

1- يقدم طلب الزواج لقاضي المنطقة مع الوثائق الآتية:

أ ـ شهادة من مختار وعرفاء المحلة باسم كل من الخاطب والمخطوبة وسنة ومحل إقامته واسم وليه وأنه لا يمنع من هذا الزواج مانع شرعي

ب ـ صورة مصدقة عن قيد نفوس الطرفين وأحوالهما الشخصية

ج ـ شهادة من طبيب يختاره الطرفان بخلوهما من الأمراض السارية ومن الموانع الصحية للزواج، وللقاضي التثبت من ذلك بمعرفة طبيب يختاره

د ـ رخصة بالزواج للعسكريين ولمن هم في سن الجندية الإجبارية

هـ ـ موافقة مديرية الأمن العام إن كان أحد الزوجين أجنبياً

2- لا يجوز تثبيت الزواج المعقود خارج المحكمة إلا بعد استيفاء هذه الإجراءات على أنه إذا حصل ولد أو حمل ظاهر يثبت الزواج بدون هذه الإجراءات ولا يمنع ذلك من إيقاع العقوبة القانونية

المادة 41

- يأذن القاضي بإجراء العقد فوراً بعد استكمال هذه الوثائق وله عند الاشتباه تأخيره لإعلانه مدة عشرة أيام والقاضي يختار طريقة الإعلان

المادة 42

ـ إذا لم يجر العقد خلال ستة أشهر يعتبر الإذن ملغى معاملات العقد

المادة 43

ـ يقوم القاضي أو من يأذن له من مساعدي المحكمة بإجراء العقد

المادة 44

ـ يجب أن يشمل صك الزواج:

أ ـ أسماء الطرفين كاملة وموطن كل منهما

ب ـ وقوع العقد وتاريخه ومكانه

ج ـ أسماء الشهود والوكلاء كاملة وموطن كل منهم

د ـ مقدار المهر المعجل والمؤجل وهل قبض المعجل أم لا

هـ ـ توقيع أصحاب العلاقة والمأذون وتصديق القاضي

المادة 45

1- يسجل المساعد الزواج في سجله المخصوص ويبعث بصورة عنه لدائرة الأحوال المدنية خلال عشرة أيام من تاريخ الزواج

2- تغني هذه الصورة عن إخبار الطرفين دائرة الأحوال المدنية بالزواج ويكون المساعد مسئولا عن إهمال إرسال الصورة

3- تطبق الطريقة نفسها في تسجيل الأحكام الصادرة بتثبيت الزواج والطلاق والنسب ووفاة المفقود، ويقوم أمين السجل المدني بتدوين ذلك في السجلات المخصوصة دون حاجة إلى أي إجراء آخر

المادة 46

ـ تعفى معاملات الزواج من كل رسم

الكتاب الثاني. انحلال الزواج

المادة 95

-: 1- يشترط لصحة المخالعة أن يكون الزوج أهلاً لإيقاع الطلاق والمرآة محلاً له

2- المرآة التي لم تبلغ سن الرشد إذا خولعت لا تلتزم ببدل الخلع إلا بموافقة ولي المال

المادة 96

ـ لكل من الطرفين الزوجون عن إيجابه في المخالعة قبل قبول الآخر

المادة 97

ـ كل ما صح التزامه شرعاً صلح أن يكون بدلاً في الخلع

المادة 98

ـ إذا كانت المخالعة على مال غير المهر لزم أداؤه وبرئت ذمة المتخالعين من كل حق يتعلق بالمهر والنفقة الزوجية

المادة 99

ـ إذا لم يسم المتخالعان شيئاً وقت المخالعة برئ كل منهما من حقوق الآخر بالمهر والنفقة الزوجية

المادة 100

ـ إذا صرح المتخالعان بنفي البدل كانت المخالعة في حكم الطلاق المحض ووقع بها طلقة رجعية

المادة 101

ـ نفقة العدة لا تسقط ولا يبرأ الزوج المخالع منها إلا إذا نص عليها صراحة في عقد المخالعة

المادة 102

ـ: 1ـ إذا اشترط في المخالعة إعفاء الزوج من أجرة إرضاع الولد أو اشترط إمساك أمه له مدة معلومة وإنفاقها عليه فتزوجت أو تركت الولد يرجع

الزوج على الزوجة بما يعادل أجرة رضاع الولد أو نفقته عن المدة الباقية

2ـ إذا كانت الأم معسرة وقت المخالعة أو أعسرت فيما بعد يجبر الأب على نفقة الولد وتكون دينا له على الأم

المادة 103

ـ إذا اشترط الرجل في المخالعة إمساك الولد عنده مدة الحضانة صحت المخالعة وبطل الشرط وكان لحاضنته الشرعية أخذه منه ويلزم أبوه بنفقته

وأجرة حضانته إن كان الولد فقيراً

المادة 104

ـ لا يجري التقاص بين نفقة الولد المستحقة على أبيه ودين الأب على الحاضنة

SYRIAN CONSTITUTION (EXTRACTS)

The following extracts are taken from Part 1 — Basic Principles — of the Syrian Constitution:

English Translation

Chapter 2. Economic Principles

Article 17 [Inheritance]
The right of inheritance is guaranteed in accordance with the law.

Chapter 4. Freedom, Rights, Duties

Article 44 [Family, Marriage, Children]
(1) The family is the basic unit of society and is protected by the state.

(2) The state protects and encourages marriage and eliminates the material and social obstacles hindering it. The state protects mothers and infants and extends care to adolescents and youths and provides them with the suitable circumstances to develop their faculties.

Article 45 [Women]
The state guarantees women all opportunities enabling them to fully and effectively participate in the political, social, cultural, and economic life. The state removes the restrictions that prevent women's development and participation in building the socialist Arab society.

Article 46 [Insurance, Welfare]

(1) The state insures every citizen and his family in cases of emergency, illness, disability, orphan-hood, and old age.

(2) The state protects the citizens' health and provides them with the means of protection, treatment, and medication.

Article 47 [Services]

The state guarantees cultural, social, and health services. It especially undertakes to provide these services to the village in order to raise its standard.

Article 48 [Organizations]

The popular sectors have the right to establish unionist, social, professional organizations, and production cooperatives. The framework of the organizations, their relations, and the scope of their work is defined by law.

Article 49 [Organizational Functions]

The popular organizations by law effectively participate in the various sectors and councils to realize the following:

(1) Building the socialist Arab society and defending the system.

(2) Planning and guiding of the socialist economy.

(3) Development of work conditions, safety, health, culture, and all other affairs pertaining to the lives of the organization members.

(4) Achievement of scientific and technical progress and the development of the means of production.

(5) Popular supervision of the machinery of government.

الفصل الثاني: المبادئ الاقتصادية

المادة السابعة عشر

حق الإرث مضمون وفقاً للقانون.

الفصل الرابع: الحريات والحقوق والواجبات العامة

المادة الرابعة والأربعون

1- الأسرة هي خلية المجتمع الأساسية وتحميها الدولة.

2- تحمي الدولة الزواج وتشجع عليه وتعمل على إزالة العقبات المادية والاجتماعية التي تعوقه وتحمي الأمومة والطفولة وترعى النشء والشباب وتوفر لهم الظروف المناسبة لتنمية ملكاتهم.

المادة الخامسة والأربعون

تكفل الدولة للمرأة جميع الفرص التي تتيح لها المساهمة الفعالة والكاملة في الحياة السياسية والاجتماعية والثقافية والاقتصادية وتعمل على إزالة القيود التي تمنع تطورها ومشاركتها في بناء المجتمع العربي الاشتراكي.

المادة السادسة والأربعون

1- تكفل الدولة كل مواطن وأسرته في حالات الطوارئ والمرض والعجز واليتم والشيخوخة.

2- تحمي الدولة صحة المواطنين وتوفر لهم وسائل الوقاية والمعالجة والتداوي.

المادة السابعة والأربعون

تكفل الدولة الخدمات الثقافية والاجتماعية والصحية وتعمل بوجه خاص على توفيرها للقرية رفعا لمستواها.

المادة الثامنة والأربعون

للقطاعات الجماهيرية حق إقامة تنظيمات نقابية أو اجتماعية أو مهنية أو جمعيات تعاونية للإنتاج أو الخدمات وتحدد القوانين إطار التنظيمات وعلاقاتها وحدود عملها.

المادة التاسعة والأربعون

تشارك التنظيمات الجماهيرية مشاركة فعالة في مختلف القطاعات والمجالس المحددة بالقوانين في تحقيق الأمور التالية:

1- بناء المجتمع العربي الاشتراكي وحماية نظامه.

2- تخطيط وقيادة الاقتصاد الاشتراكي.

3- تطوير شروط العمل والوقاية والصحة والثقافة وجميع الشؤون الأخرى المرتبطة بحياة أفرادها.

4- تحقيق التقدم العلمي والتقني وتطوير أساليب الإنتاج .

5- الرقابة الشعبية على أجهزة الحكم.

BIBLIOGRAPHY

Ali, Abdullah Yusuf (trans.), *The Holy Quran: English Translation of the Meanings* (Fahd Holy Quran Printing Complex: 1987).

Bureau of Near Eastern Affairs, U.S. Department of State, "Background Note: Syria," available at http://www.state.gov/r/pa/ei/bgn/3580.htm.

Central Intelligence Agency, "Syria," *The World Factbook*, available at https://www.cia.gov/library/publications/the-world-factbook/geos/sy.html.

Constitution of the Syrian Arabic Republic of 1973 and Explanations (دستور الجمهورية العربية السورية و تعديلاته).

Decree number 76 dated Sep. 26, 2010 to amend article 308 of the code of the Code of Personal Status (أصدر الرئيس (76) تاريخ 2010/9/26 قضي بتعديل المادة بشار الأسد المرسوم رقم قانون الأحوال الشخصية النافذ حالياً والمتعلقة بالطوائف 308 من المسيحية واليهودية.)

Embassy of the United States in Syria, "Adoption: Information on International Adoptions," available at http://damascus.usembassy.gov/adoption.html.

Faruqi, Harith Suleiman, *Faruqi's Law Dictionary (Arabic-English; English-Arabic)*, Librairie du Liban Publishers الفاروقي، حارث سليمان، المعجم القانوني (عربي- (Beirut: 1983). إنكليزي؛ إنكليزي-عربي)، مكتبة لبنان(بيروت: 1983).

Info-Prod Research (Middle East) Ltd., "Syria: Judiciary," available at: http://www.infoprod.co.il/country/syria2a.htm.

Interview with Souhail Abou-Rass, attorney in private practice in Damascus, Syria. 11 November 2010.

Interview with Daad Mousa, attorney in private practice in Damascus, Syria. 14 November 2010.

Interview with Yamman Samman, attorney in private practice in Damascus, Syria. 10 November 2010.

Personal Status Law of the Catholic Communities in Syria no. 31 of 2006 (قانون الأحوال الشخصية للطوائف الكاثوليكية في سورية - قانون رقم 31 لعام 2006، إعداد وتنسيق الأب أنطون مصلح).

Syrian Ministry of Interior's Office of Civil Affairs web site, available at http://www.civilaffair-moi.gov.sy/sf04/index.php?lang=ar&page=ar_civiliza tion.htm.

Syrian Personal Status Law (قانون الأحوال لشخصية، الصادر بالمرسوم التشريعي رقم / 90 / لعام 1953، و مذكرته الا يضاحية).

Unclassified Damascus Briefing 00000657, VZCZCXYZ0000, RR RUEHWEB. FM American Embassy Damascus. E.O. 13526.

United States Embassy in Damascus, Consular Sections Sharepoint site, available at.